ORGANIZE!

A Manual for Leaders

by Dean Brackley

Paulist Press
New York/Mahwah, N.J.

Book design by Faces Type & Design.

Library of Congress Cataloging-in-Publication Data

Brackley, Dean.
    Organize! : a manual for leaders / by Dean Brackley.
       p.   cm.
    ISBN 0-8091-3176-5
    1. Church work with the poor—Catholic Church—Handbooks, manuals, etc.
2. Church work with the poor—New York (N.Y.)—Handbooks, manuals, etc.
3. Church and social problems—Catholic Church—Handbooks, manuals, etc.
4. Catholic Church—New York (N.Y.)—History. 5. New York (N.Y.)—Church history. 6. South Bronx (New York, N.Y.)—Church history. 7. South Bronx People for Change.
    I. Title.
    BX2347.8.P66B73   1990
    254′.6—dc20
                                                              90-35838
                                                              CIP

Published by Paulist Press
997 Macarthur Boulevard
Mahwah, New Jersey 07430

Printed and bound in the
United States of America

Contents

Introduction 1

PART I: BASIC CONCEPTS 5
            1. Power 6
            2. Social Action 9

PART II: YOUR GROUP 11
            1. Group Meetings 12
            2. Leading a Discussion 18
            3. Leadership 20
            4. The Leadership Team 22
            5. Phone Tree 23
            6. Group Check List .24

PART III: ORGANIZING—Ten Key Steps 25
            1. Exploring the Neighborhood 27
            2. Recruiting 29
               a. Personal Contact 30
               b. Make a List 31
               c. "Door-Knocking" 33
               d. Interviews (House Visits) 36
               e. Speaking to a Group 38
            3. Picking an Issue .39
            4. Research the Issue 42
            5. Strategy: Plan Your Campaign 46
            6. Getting Support .49
            7. Publicity 50
            8. The Action 54
               a. Tactics 55
               b. Public Meetings 59
               c. Negotiation 63
            9. Evaluation 66
            10. Monitor the Agreement 67
            11. Celebrate! 67

Introduction

Organize! is the leadership training manual of South Bronx People for Change, a church-based community organizing project begun in 1979. The manual has been newly expanded and directed to a wider audience. As the song says, "If we can make it *there,* we'll make it anywhere. . . ." Not that we've actually made it in the South Bronx—not by a long shot! But a unique *spirit* stamps social action there in a way that is worth sharing.

A plague of abandonment—by banks, landlords, and government—eventually wrecked South Bronx neighborhoods in the late 1960s and 1970s. It destroyed over 100,000 housing units and displaced more than 250,000 persons. Never before had such destruction taken place apart from war or natural disaster. Maybe it *was* war. It left the area more thoroughly disorganized and more dependent than ever.

EMPOWERING PEOPLE When everything else came undone in the 1970s, many church congregations responded generously, supplying social services and even developing housing for afflicted neighbors. The most far-sighted people soon realized, however, that the greatest challenge was to develop the area's richest resource, its *people.* Only people power could break the dependency. As the Catholic bishops would later state in their pastoral letter on the U.S. economy: "Poor people must be empowered to take charge of their own futures and become responsible for their own economic advancement" (no. 201). So, in the mid-1970s laypeople and church workers planned People for Change as an organization of the people and by the people.

The new project would combine (1) community organizing, (2) analysis of local power, and (3) faith reflection. Training in organizing would provide skills for tackling problems like poor public services and heatless apartments in the winter. Organizing would help develop local power.

With power analysis, people could draw back the curtains that hide the levers of local and city power. But this conscientization had to stress *values* as well as knowledge. Otherwise, social change could become just another changing of the guard. No more secret plans! No more corrupt leaders!

Opening a space for religious expression *within* social action was a matter of simple respect for a people that believes deeply and has not learned the difficult trick of separating faith from everyday life. And yet unlocking the power of faith in the struggle for justice proved a stiff challenge from the beginning. Many creative efforts, such as the Sunday afternoon scripture reflections, have since helped people express the social meaning of their faith for today.

In the early days, Chicago priest Larry Gorman contributed to this effort, while Sr. Marge Tuite provided local leaders with tools for power analysis. People for Change embraced Margie's inspiring vision, summarized below (page 8). (*People Power* develops this in greater detail in comic book form. *People Power* and the companion booklet *Group Exercises with "People Power,"* both written by the present author, are available from Paulist Press.)

Harry Fagan trained People for Change's first organizers. His approach to social action has stamped struggles over housing, utility rates, and crime control for over ten years. *Organize!* owes a deep debt to Harry and his wonderful book *Empowerment* (Paulist Press, 1979) both for its organization and even its language (see below: "Power," "The Leadership Team," "Getting Concrete and Specific," "Research," and "Getting Support"). Many other hands have also shaped *Organize!,* especially the People for Change staff and volunteer trainers who have worked to improve the training program over the years. The lively drawings of our gifted neighbor Joey Negron have long brightened our training handouts. Now they grace this book.

FOR LOCAL LEADERS *Organize!* explains social action skills to local leaders. The basic unit of the People for Change organization is a core group of leaders rooted in a local neighborhood and attached to a local church. *Organize!* is designed to help train such a team to mobilize the local community to deal with its problems. This purpose divides the book into three parts: Part I explains basic concepts and values related to social action. Part II shows how to organize and maintain a local social action group. Part III explains how to mount action campaigns to resolve community issues.

Since it is directed to local leaders, the present book does not include everything an organizer must do to build a *people's organization.* It says nothing about long-range planning, financial support, or launching an organization in the community. For this kind of information, consult a trained organizer or the many fine books addressed to these topics.

Besides our own experience and *Empowerment,* we have drawn on many such books here, including Si Kahn's *Organizing* (McGraw-Hill, 1982), Shel Trapp's *Dynamics of Organizing* (NTIC), and Roger Hayes' series of booklets *Workshops in Organizing* (Community Organizing Unit, CSS, 1985). Each develops in its own way the tradition of Saul Alinsky who spelled out the basic principles of community organizing in two classic works, *Reveille for Radicals* and *Rules for Radicals* (Random House, 1969 and 1972).

OUR SECRET WEAPON

Sin abounds in the South Bronx—but grace does more abound. If poverty and destruction have brought frustration and addiction, they have also shaped a generation of tireless survivors who cling to what is important in life. Generosity, hard work, humor, compassion, faith, and fiesta flourish more than crime in the South Bronx. The majority, after all, work hard, struggling to raise decent families against the odds. They draw their warmth and strength from the rich cultural soil of the Caribbean and the rural south. New York street savvy blends with this heritage in their struggle for justice.

In time, emphasis on participation, values, and faith at People for Change has allowed the people to shape their struggle for justice into an expression of their own tough and tender spirit. People for Change turns this spirit loose in the streets.

South Bronx people have shown young turks and outsiders that you don't have to lie or manipulate people in order to succeed—and that winning-at-any-price is unworthy of us. They reject violence, and even disrespect for the officials who show such disrespect for them. They have taught us that we need not humiliate the powerful, even as we debunk their pretensions. We don't coerce opponents, we pressure them. And when we confront them, as we frequently must, our only weapon is the truth. We have learned from the people the importance of Gandhi's truth-force and the centrality of respect for persons. Small wonder that the wisdom of Martin Luther King, Jr. has had a growing impact on our organization.

"That's our secret weapon," said one pastor when senior citizen Mary Cummins hugged and kissed "the enemy," the Bronx police commander. The secret weapon surfaced again when school children sang hymns for a startled Housing Commissioner and pleaded for housing for the poor. Victoria Santos also unsheathed the secret weapon when she trained her picture of Jesus on the cops and bolted doors which sought to block our entrance to housing headquarters downtown.

The people have shown us how to be patient but to never give up. They have taught us the importance of humor and song, of prayer and celebration, no matter how grave the cause or grim the hour. They know that we are crazy to work for a new Bronx without God's help, and they have shown us how to speak God's name without embarrassment in the heat of the battle. In short, they have taught us to maintain our humanity in the fight for social justice.

This book is dedicated to the staff members and trainers of South Bronx People for Change over the years, especially to Angel Garcia and Mildred Bonilla, Blanca Ramirez, Vilma Silva, Marilu

Fermaintt, and Mark Colville—tireless and generous workers who embody the South Bronx spirit.

Besides them, Ed Dunn and Joe Hacala have recently provided important suggestions for improving this book. Special thanks are also due to the Woodstock Theological Center in Washington, D.C. for the opportunity to put *Organize!* into final form.

Dean Brackley
July 16, 1989

Organize! has a companion booklet, *Workshops with "Organize!"* (Paulist Press, 1990) by the same author. It contains workshop plans and other resources for developing a training program using *Organize!*

PART I: BASIC CONCEPTS

Social action is about power—people power, to be exact. It is easy to misunderstand both social action and power. Many confuse social action with social service or community development. Many confuse people power with other kinds of power.

The next few pages should help you and your group clarify your thinking and work toward a common vision about the kind of action that can give you and your neighbors more control over what happens in your local community.

PART I has two sections:

1. Power = People + Knowledge
2. Social Action

1. POWER

From the very beginning we must think clearly about power. Otherwise, we can lose sight of the **values** that inspire our social action in the first place. These are rooted in our deepest beliefs and the traditions inspired by the Bible.

There can be no brotherhood and sisterhood without **social justice.** But social justice demands a fair distribution of **power.** In social action, we seek and use power to bring about the justice that makes real **community** possible.

"Now power properly understood is nothing but the ability to achieve purpose. It is the strength required to bring about social, political and economic change. . . .

"There is nothing wrong with power if power is used correctly. . . .

"Now, we've got to get this thing right. What is needed is a realization that power without love is reckless and abusive, and love without power is sentimental and anemic. Power at its best is love implementing the demands of justice, and justice at its best is power correcting everything that stands against love. And this is what we must see as we move on."

—Martin Luther King, Jr.
Final SCLC Presidential Address

POWER Is the Ability to Get Things Done

- Like everything else God has created:
  Power can be used to do *good* . . . or for *evil*.
  (Can you think of examples of each?)

- You can have *selfish* power: power *over* others:
  (Where have you experienced this?)

  You can have *shared* power: power *with* others:
  (Where have you experienced this?)

- Power can *keep* things the way they are: (Give examples.)

  Power can *change* things.      (Give examples.)

THERE ARE MANY KINDS OF POWER. LIST AS MANY AS YOU CAN:

1. _____ Money _____,
2. _____,
3. _____,
4. _____.

We want the kind of power that corresponds to human dignity. Power **to change things.** Power **shared with others.** Power that makes **love** effective in the community. We want:

PEOPLE POWER!

We rely on the power of the **TRUTH** and the dignity of **PEOPLE.** So we define power like this:

POWER = PEOPLE + KNOWLEDGE

where **"People"** means **constituency** and includes groups and institutions.

We base our understanding of power and social action on the **social philosophy,** or vision, of South Bronx People for Change. We present this on the next page. It seeks to reflect for today the **social values** that are central to the message of the Bible.

People Power

As we see it, there are **three ways** people can relate to each other:

1. AS UNEQUALS.

One person has **power over** another,

makes decisions **for** them,

keeps them **dependent**,

—but doesn't have to **answer to** them!

2. IGNORING EACH OTHER.

People **share** neither their problems nor their dreams,

seek **private solutions** to common problems,

and **compete** where they could cooperate.

3. AS EQUALS.

People **depend on** each other

and **answer to** each other.

In this soil of **respect**, trust and love can grow!

When people act like this, they make up **groups** and **institutions** that look like these—

1. The PYRAMID.

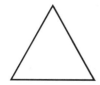

Here a few at the top have **power over** the many at the bottom,

keep them **dependent**,

make **decisions for** them,

—but don't have to **answer to** them!!

No real **participation**.

A climate of **fear and anxiety**.

2. The CROWD.

Disorganized groups, easily pushed around.

Where? At the bottom of the pyramid.

Splits: Black vs. White vs. Latino. Women vs. men. Young vs. old. Etc.

Climate: **distrust** and **lack of hope**.

3. The TEAM (Circle).

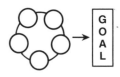

A group of equals seeking a **common goal**.

They **depend on** each other,

share power, decisions and information.

They don't compete, they **cooperate**.

They answer to the **goal**.

Climate: **creative tension**.

* See Dean Brackley, *People Power* (Paulist Press, 1989). Illustrated by Larry Nolte.

2. SOCIAL ACTION

What is it anyway?

Let's compare SOCIAL ACTION to SOCIAL SERVICE . . .

SOCIAL SERVICE	SOCIAL ACTION
• Deals with needs and problems of *individuals*.	• Deals with policies of social *institutions* (bank, education, government, etc.).
• You do something *FOR* someone.	• You do something *WITH* someone.
• One-to-one.	• Group.
• Charity.	• Justice.
• Deals with *effects*.	• Deals with *causes*.
• No social *change*.	• Works for *change*.
• Does not build *power*.	• Builds *power*.
• Danger: Dependency without accountability or empowerment. Client and expert.	• Danger?

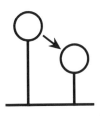

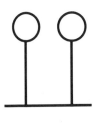

People who do social action are usually kind and generous. They easily can *drift* into social service. Not a bad thing at all. But let's be clear. WE ARE INTERESTED HERE IN SOCIAL ACTION.

AN EXERCISE: *What Would You Do?*

SCENARIO #1

Recently an abandoned car and heavy refuse (furniture, etc.) have been dumped on the side of the road near the park. People are very upset. They have called the police and the sanitation department, but the junk is still there. One of your friends suggests taking up a collection from neighbors to have the car privately towed and the junk removed.

What would you do?

SCENARIO #2

An angry man contacts your group and says he was robbed of his paycheck after he cashed it at the local bank. He also knows of others who have been mugged leaving the bank. He wants to know: "What will the group do about the muggings?"

How would you handle this?

SCENARIO #3

It is January. A building nearby has not had heat for three weeks. The prospects for heat look dim for the rest of the winter.
A few tenants from the building visit you and your group for help. They want to move out and they want you to help them look for warm apartments.

What do you do?

PART II: YOUR GROUP

In order to drive from one city to another, you not only need to know how to drive and how to get there; you need a car in good working order. In the same way, in order to organize your community, you not only need to know how to do social action; you need to keep your social action group in good running order. Part II will help you keep your group in good running order. Then you can "drive" it all over—and build people power in your community.

PART II has six sections:

1. **Group Meetings**
2. **Leading a Discussion**
3. **Leadership**
4. **The Leadership Team**
5. **Phone Tree**
6. **Group Check List**

1. GROUP MEETINGS

A good social action group should meet regularly, at least once a month. But bad meetings kill good groups. This section will help you run brief, productive meetings, where members participate and don't just observe.

DOWN WITH LONG, BORING MEETINGS!!

Question: Why have meetings in the first place?

Answer: *To plan action.*

To socialize, throw a party. To share information, telephone or send out a newsletter. Have a meeting **to plan an action**—recruitment, a demonstration, a dance, etc.

In general, meetings should go one hour or a little more. A meeting that does not go all night should **focus on just one thing.** Plan **one** action per meeting. We call this focus the **MAJOR ISSUE** of the meeting.

Don't start from scratch at the meeting. The leadership team (at least two members) brings a **PROPOSAL FOR ACTION** to the meeting and presents it to members. (For example: "We propose that the group invite the head of the Sanitation Department to a meeting in the neighborhood so we can get rid of the abandoned cars being dumped across from the school.")

Leaders propose an action to save time, not to push their own ideas. Members can then accept the proposal, reject it, or change it. The leaders might even bring a list of jobs for the action they propose—as long as they don't force their ideas on the group.

Of course, this means that the group leaders have to meet beforehand to plan the agenda for the group meeting. This earlier "leadership meeting" should be open to all members.

At the beginning of the group meeting, leaders present **THE AGENDA** to everyone for approval. Members can accept, reject, or change the agenda. (So it's a good idea for leaders to seek advice on the agenda from key members before the meeting.) Once members approve the agenda it becomes **theirs**, and members give the chairperson responsibility for seeing that **the people's agenda** is followed.

This is a big relief for chairpersons! They don't have to defend their own authority. Their job is to **defend the group's agenda.** The agenda really runs the meeting: "Finish up, Sally. We agreed to come to a decision by 8:30—unless the group wants to change the agenda."

You might have a second issue, a **MINOR ISSUE**, to discuss. Give it 10 minutes, 15 at most. This means serious discussion and work on the minor issue has to take place before or after the group meeting. For example: A minor issue might be a report and decision about a project—say, voter registration—that is **already in progress.** Or it might be a new project which you can give to a committee to work on **after** the group meeting. To save time, the group could give this committee the authority to make decisions about the issue without calling everybody together.

A meeting should have some **OPEN TIME** so people don't feel that the agenda is a straightjacket. Use open time for new business and as an "escape valve" so that surprises don't destroy your agenda: "This afternoon, Marge's grandmother died. Let's set aside our open time to talk about that."

Time to **SOCIALIZE** before or after the meeting helps glue the group together.

The following page shows how a regular group meeting is structured. The heart of the meeting is the **three D's:**

Discuss the proposal for action.

Decide on the action.

Division of labor for the action.

Study the page carefully.

The two pages after that talk about running meetings. Then follows an exercise on how to **prepare an agenda** at a **leadership meeting.** The next section deals with leading discussions and bringing the group to decisions.

The Agenda

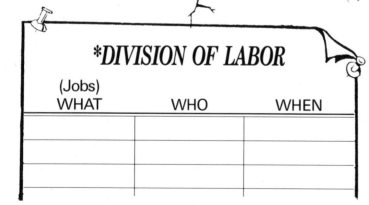

AGENDA

1. **REFLECTION**
2. **APPROVE AGENDA**
3. **MINUTES**

4. **MAJOR ISSUE**—25 min.
   (A Proposal for Action)

   —DISCUSS

   —DECIDE

   —DIVISION OF LABOR*

5. *MINOR ISSUE*—10 min.
6. **OPEN TIME**—10 min.
7. **SUMMARY** (Chairperson)
8. **ADJOURN**

*DIVISION OF LABOR

(Jobs) WHAT	WHO	WHEN

Call a meeting to decide an **ACTION.**

- **REFLECTION:**
  Prayer, reflection on faith or on the values that brought us here and keep us going.

- **MAJOR ISSUE:**
  An action meeting that doesn't go all night must have a single focus, **a major issue.**

- Present a **PROPOSAL FOR ACTION** about the major issue. **Discuss** it, **decide** on it, **divide up** jobs (see below).

- **MINOR ISSUE:**
  If you treat another issue, make it a minor issue.
  a. Report on a project in progress;
  b. Appoint a committee to work on a new project; etc.
  Serious discussion and work on this issue must be done at some other time.

- **OPEN TIME:**
  Freedom for participants. Escape valve for emergencies and surprises.

- **SUMMARY:**
  Accomplishments of the meeting, jobs to be done, encouragement, next steps, etc.

- **ADJOURN:**
  Prayer, song, refreshments, etc.

- **DIVISION OF LABOR:**
  Assign jobs during the meeting. Otherwise, it's all worthless.

Running the Group Meeting

BEFORE THE MEETING

☐ Inform the members.

☐ Leadership meeting (see "Preparing a Group Meeting," below).
  • Plan the time, place, and purpose of the group meeting
  • Prepare the agenda

☐ Share the agenda with other key people. (Mail to members?)

☐ Recruit. Give jobs to do at the meeting (set up).

DURING THE MEETING

☐ Don't string out membership.

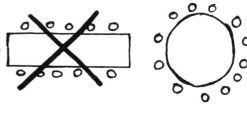

☐ Use a sign-up sheet.

☐ Post the agenda right near the chairperson.
  (Or give a copy to everybody.)

☐ Begin on time; end on time.
  (People who come late should miss *something*.)

☐ Decide together when you want to finish the meeting.
  The meeting should not last much more than one hour.

☐ Present the agenda to all for their approval.

☐ Have a *CHAIRPERSON* to "run" the meeting by *protecting the agenda.*

The *AGENDA* really runs the meeting!!

The chairperson:

—gets *everybody to participate,* inviting the shy to speak, gently but firmly keeping individuals from dominating.

—brings the group to *a decision about action.*

☐ Have a *RECORDER* (or SECRETARY) take notes for minutes.

☐ Have as many people as possible do things: one person to do the prayer, another to present the minor issue, another the major issue, etc.

☐ *Everyone* should leave with at least one *job* to do.

AFTER THE MEETING

☐ Evaluate with leadership.

☐ Cheerlead with membership and others. There's no such thing as a bad meeting.

☐ The RECORDER calls later on to remind people to do their jobs.

☐ Somebody calls "old faithfuls" who didn't show up.

AN EXERCISE: *Preparing a Group Meeting*

This is the situation before the group meeting:

1. Your group needs to **raise $1,000** over the next three months.

   The group wants to reserve the school hall for a fundraiser event. To reserve the busy hall, you'll have to inform the pastor by *next Monday*.

2. The **voter registration campaign** has started. Group members are registering voters. The campaign ends *in four weeks*, and to meet your goal you need to get an update on how many people have been registered up to now.

3. The group just found out some surprising news: The local public official responsible for your area wants to get **two abandoned buildings demolished** in your neighborhood. Your group wanted to *seal* them up to save them.

   There are *two months* before the demolition contract is signed.

4. Your group has arranged to meet *in one week* with key **police officials** about serious narcotics trafficking in your area.

QUESTIONS

A. Which of the above matters can you take care of *outside* of the group meeting?   ☐

B. Which matter is not urgent and can be handled at a later meeting?   ☐

C. Which is most urgent and needs the whole group to work on it at the group meeting?   ☐
   (This will be the MAJOR ISSUE of the meeting.)

D. Which can you prepare well and take care of in 10 minutes at the meeting?   ☐
   (This will be the MINOR ISSUE in the group meeting.)

2. LEADING A DISCUSSION

Here are some general pointers about how to lead a discussion, followed by some remarks on group decision making.

1. The discussion leader's job is to foster broad active **participation** and to **focus** and **guide** the dialogue—not to give a lot of input.

2. Everybody should feel **included** and **invited** to speak. Some people need an invitation—but one that leaves them free and not threatened.

3. When people talk too much, remind them gently but firmly that others have not had the chance to speak much yet, that someone got cut off, or that we ought to follow up on what another person just said.

4. Everyone's ideas should be **respected.** This does not mean, though, that we all have to agree. Exploring disagreements can be very fruitful.

5. Invite people to develop further what they said.

6. Help participants connect what one person says to what others have already said: "Didn't Maria say something like that . . . ?" Always try to **deepen** the discussion by building on what has been said already.

7. Every now and then—and especially when the discussion has drifted or lost focus—give a brief **summary** of the basic ideas touched on so far. Then offer a question that can give the discussion a new focus and direction.

8. Instead of questions that expect a "Yes" or "No" answer, ask questions that invite participants to speak more: "What do you think . . . ?" "Why . . . ?" "How . . . ?" "Did something like that ever happen to anyone here?" "What caught your attention?" "Why?"

9. **Pass the ball.** You don't have to answer questions addressed to you. Often it is better to ask others to tackle them: "Does anyone want to comment on what Paul just said?" "Veronica, do you?"

10. Is it time to move on? Say so.

11. One person should speak at a time. If three people want to talk, order the responses. "OK, how about first Millie, then Ralph, then Marilyn?"

12. The more active participation the better. Have participants split up into small groups, even into pairs, to discuss a question for, say, three minutes. Then they can come back together and share their conclusions. These can be posted for all to see and to promote further discussion. (Just write *key words,* not sentences.) People generally like their ideas posted like this.

13. Sometimes, at the end of a discussion, it might not be clear whether we got anywhere. Summarize the main points one last time with the help of participants. You'll be surprised!

Group Decision Making

Don't **VOTE** on serious matters unless you have to. Voting means there are **losers.** Use voting: (1) for matters of little importance, or (2) when you **have** to make a decision in a short time, or (3) when there are large numbers of people.

Try to get **CONSENSUS.** Search for **the decision most people favor and that _everyone_ can support** even if it's not their favorite.

- Participants present pros and cons of various positions. Write on newsprint or chalkboard if necessary. Urge participants not to try to **win arguments** but to **search together** for the best solution. Encourage all **to speak and to listen.**

- Explore differences; don't bury them. People will support what the group decides **if** their own views have been **heard and respected: "People will support what they help to create"** (Lawson, Griffin, and Donant, _Leadership Is Everybody's Business,_ San Luis Obispo, Cal.: Impact Publishers, 1976, p. 128).

- Say: "It seems most people favor X. Is that right? Is X our decision?"

- Have the group try to answer and accommodate objections to X. Ask: "Is anyone still strongly opposed?" Ask "**holdouts**" if they will go along with the decision if everyone else wants it—or if no one else strongly opposes it.

All the points touched on here are too much to carry around in your head. Don't try to remember them all when you are in the middle of a discussion. Instead, review these pages _after_ each discussion to see how you did. Leading a good discussion takes skill. With practice and review, you can learn well in a short time.

3. LEADERSHIP

You can't have social change without leaders. Unfortunately, when they hear the word "leader," most people think of either a dictator ("the BOSS") or a Martin Luther King. We don't want dictators, and we don't have many Martin Luther Kings. So what does leadership mean to us?

Leaders are just **regular people** who help the group serve the community. **Leaders are servants, not dictators.** And anyone can serve—even if one is not Martin Luther King.

Most leaders are made, not born. People can learn how to lead (serve) and still be themselves. There are many leadership styles. Each one should find the style that makes one feel most comfortable.

Whatever their style, leaders **inspire others with a vision of how things can be different,** and they help others make that vision real.

Therefore:

- Leaders are **COMMUNICATORS.** They are sensitive and understanding. Leaders **listen.** They bring other people in. They are open to all types and groups of people.

- Leaders are **ENTHUSIASTIC.** They give hope to others.

- Finally, leaders are **TEAM BUILDERS.** They help all to **participate democratically** and use their talents. They help **overcome conflicts** in the group, and they move the group to **action.**

This is **democratic leadership.** Democratic leadership respects other people. It is based on the philosophy of **People Power** (see page 8).

See, on the next page, what a difference it makes!

Democratic Leadership
—What a Difference!

NOT:

BUT: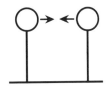

LEADERSHIP is not a personality.
The leader is **not** "the BOSS."

LEADERSHIP is many JOBS:
planning, inspiring, taking care of people, etc. Your group can have **many leaders.**

The leader does **not** do all the work.

Leaders help **everyone** work **together.**

The group does **not** work for the leader.

The group works for its own **goal.**

The leader does **not** choose the goal.

The group chooses the goal.

The group does **not** answer to the leader(s).

Leaders help the group answer to the **goal.**

Leaders are **not** the only ones responsible for success and failure.

Everyone is responsible for success and failure.

The leader does **not** control information.

The group shares information.

The leader does **not** control power.

The group shares power.

The leader does **not** make all the decisions.

The group makes its own decisions. Leaders help.

The leader does **not** have all the ideas or do all the talking.

Leaders help **everyone** talk and share ideas. Leaders listen a lot.

Leaders **must** take the initiative, but . . .

Everyone **can** take initiative.

NOT: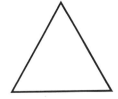

BUT: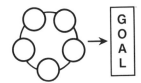

4. THE LEADERSHIP TEAM

No one person **runs** the group. Leadership has many functions. Some people are good at one, others at another.

Choose your leadership team **democratically. Rotate jobs** to give many people a sense of ownership and a chance to learn.

The functions of the LEADERSHIP TEAM are:
1. PLANNING
2. ADMINISTRATION
3. WELCOMING
4. REFLECTION

PLANNING *(COORDINATOR OR CHAIRPERSON)*

Calling the meetings.

Planning the agenda.

Chairing the meetings.

ADMINISTRATION *(SECRETARY OR RECORDER)*

Keeping the minutes of the meeting.

Keeping the group's records, files, budget, etc.

Sending notices of the meeting (starting the "phone tree"—see next page).

WELCOMING

Encouraging members.

Welcoming new people.

Socializing and refreshments.

Preparing the meeting place.

REFLECTION

Coordinating Bible (or other) reflection, prayer, song.

Note: Even functions can be divided. You could have one person keep the minutes and another keep the funds—even though both jobs are administration.

---

5. PHONE TREE

Develop a "phone tree" for your group. The first caller is the "trunk." You can have more than one trunk. You may have people in your group who can make ten calls. Great! The tree would look different:

Notice how the later callers (people less active with the group) make just one call. Several people call back to show that the tree is working. (See *arrows*.) TEST IT!

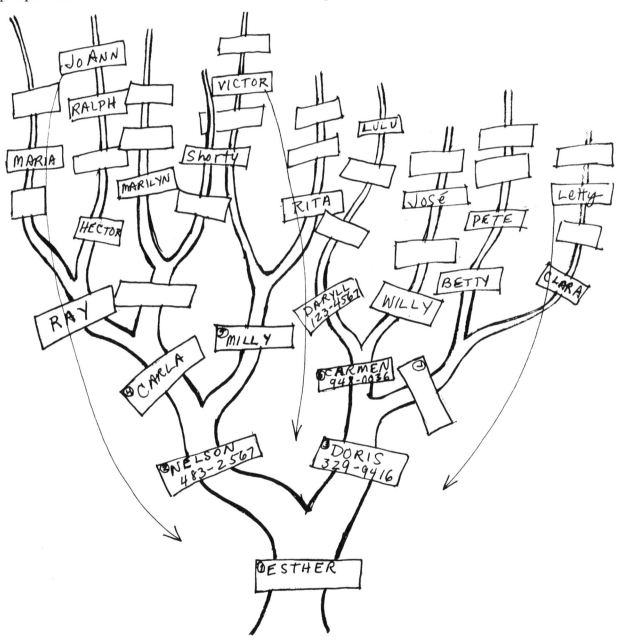

6. GROUP CHECK LIST

Your group needs a number of **resources** and **skills** to be able to run like a well-built car. Check them off:

☐ The group has organized a **"phone tree"** and members can quickly share information.

☐ The group has a **community file** with **cards** of:
   1. members
   2. local groups (churches, block clubs, etc.)

☐ The group has a **directory of local agencies,** leaders, and public officials. (See page 45.)

☐ The group has local **maps** showing local school districts, community districts, fire districts, health districts, political districts, etc. (See "Exploring the Neighborhood," pages 27–28.)

☐ The group (recorder) keeps a **file** with **records, letters,** etc.

☐ The group has someone who **writes letters** and **types** them for the group.

☐ The group has access to a **duplicator.**

A group with discipline, skills, and resources is like a well-built car.
It can *go places*!
Part II has shown how to keep it running.
Part III shows how to *go places*!

PART III: ORGANIZING— TEN KEY STEPS

Part III explains the steps you take to organize and win a social action CAMPAIGN around a specific ISSUE.

1. **Exploring the Neighborhood**
2. **Recruiting**
3. **Picking an Issue**
4. **Research the Issue**
5. **Strategy: Plan Your Campaign**
6. **Getting Support**
7. **Publicity**
8. **The Action**
9. **Evaluation**
10. **Monitor the Agreement**
(and 11. **Celebrate the Victory!!**)

There's no great mystery to changing things. You just have to put some basic skills together. These ten steps are your powerful tools for tackling local problems. Sure, they take practice and hard work. But the results—and the fun—make it all worthwhile.

We present the steps in bite-size chunks and in common-sense order. For a picture of how it all fits together, take a peek at Step 5 ("Strategy"). The ten steps do not have to be learned in order. And in practice, in a real campaign, your steps will often be "out of order" and will overlap.

NOTE: The ten steps reflect the purpose of this book: training local *leaders* to tackle local problems. This section will not teach you everything an *organizer* needs to know *to build a local organization*— for example, how to begin that effort in your neighborhood or how to form coalitions with other groups. The order of the steps also follows the training needs of leaders. In the recruitment section, for example, "door-knocking" comes before "interviews" (or house visits) because door-knocking is simpler and easier to understand. In practice, interviews might come first. For example, an organizer often begins to work in a community with a campaign of interviews. Next, the organizer might gather the people interviewed for some house meetings. These house meetings usually lead up to a local assembly where people can decide what issue(s) to work on. (See the first step on the strategy diagram in Step 5.)

STEP 1: EXPLORING THE NEIGHBORHOOD

(This is a thorough check list. You won't need *all* this information at once!)

WE MUST LOOK AT THREE AREAS:

1. COMMUNITY. (Look for *trends*!)

POPULATION:

    RICH, POOR, MIDDLE-CLASS

    RACE, ETHNIC GROUPS

    AGE GROUPS (Lots of kids? Seniors?)

    UNITY? FACTIONS, DIVISIONS? ISOLATION?

HOUSING (Big landlords? Who? Homeowners? Public Housing?)

COMMERCE (Who are owners? Who are workers?)

BANKS (Community investments?)

INDUSTRY (Owners? Workers?)

PUBLIC INSTALLATIONS (Conditions?)

    STREETS
    PARKS AND PLAYGROUNDS
    LIGHTING

PUBLIC SERVICE DELIVERY

	LOCAL UNIT:	ADDRESS	PHONE	PERSON IN CHARGE	MEETINGS
COMMUNITY BOARD					
POLICE, uniformed	____PCT.				
POLICE, narcotics					
FIRE	Co.#____				
RECREATION	Dist.____				
SANITATION	Dist.____				
SCHOOLS					
PUBLIC SCHOOL DIST.					
HEALTH FACILITIES					
LOCAL POLITICIANS					

2. ORGANIZATIONS.

Put a check, or rank these organizations or give them marks.

	NAME	ADDRESS	PHONE	PERSON IN CHARGE	MTGS.	MEMBERSHIP	INTEREST IN COMMUNITY?	POWER?	WORK WITH US?	WORK AGAINST US?
CHURCHES										
TENANT ASSNS.										
BLOCK ASSNS.										
MERCHANT ASSN.										
SOCIAL SERVICE CTR. (private)										
POLITICAL CLUB, etc.										
SCHOOL (PTA)										

3. LEADERS.

"GATEKEEPERS"

OPINION LEADERS

ACTIVISTS

Now, of these leaders:
Who might work *with* us?
Who might *join* us?
Who might work *against* us?

STEP 2: RECRUITING

Introduction

Power = { People } + Knowledge

RECRUITING is the most important social action skill of all. No people, no power. No people, no social action.

Recruiting means **communicating** with people, building **trust** and **hope.** It means building **relationships**—and that is the basis of all organizing.

You can recruit someone:

1. to come to just one EVENT
   (say, a rally for better housing), OR

2. to join your CAMPAIGN about an ISSUE
   (say, to work to stop a new highway), OR

3. to JOIN YOUR GROUP OR ORGANIZATION
   (permanently, more or less).

The bigger the commitment you want, the more time you should spend recruiting someone. So recruitment comes in different shapes and sizes.

First, there's **"DOOR-KNOCKING,"** that is, stopping by for a very brief visit.

For more serious commitments, make an appointment for an **INTERVIEW,** that is, a longer friendly visit.

Finally, you can **SPEAK TO A GROUP.**

But before recruiting, remember two things: First, the key to recruitment is **PERSONAL CONTACT.** Second, plan your recruitment campaign: **MAKE A LIST.**

a. Personal Contact

PERSONAL CONTACT
IS THE REAL SECRET
TO HAVING PEOPLE JOIN YOU.

Fliers are OK . . .

. . . so are
posters . . .

Pulpit
announcements
and church bulletins
are helpful.

But all this only helps to recruit
if you are making personal contact with people.

Telephone calls
sometimes do
the trick.

BUT:

THE SECRET TO SUCCESSFUL RECRUITMENT IS PERSONAL CONTACT WITH PEOPLE!

b. Make a List

GROUP'S RECRUITMENT CAMPAIGN SHEET

RECRUITER	TARGET TO RECRUIT	ORGANIZATION	BY WHEN	ADDRESS — APT.	TELE.	COMMENTS
Sylvia	Rev. Jones	St. Mary's	this Fri.			will bring two more
Sylvia	Julio Iglesias	PTA	this Fri.			
Sylvia	Vanna White	3rd Av. Merchants	next Fri.			
Ralph	George Burns	Youth Club	this Fri.			
Ralph	Diana Ross	300 Block Club	Sun.			
Pete	Mike Tyson		this Fri.			a fighter
Pete	Bill Shakespeare		this Fri.			
Pete	F. Valenzuela		next Fri.			good with languages

"COMMENTS." INCLUDE THEIR *ISSUES* AND *CONTACTS*!

SET A CLEAR TIME-LINE AND A TIME TO MEET FOR A PROGRESS REPORT.

DECIDE HOW MANY PERSONS EACH OF YOU CAN RECRUIT FOR 1st WEEK, 2nd WEEK, ETC.

INCLUDE!

Don't forget:
• Women or Men
• Blacks, Latins, Whites, or others
• English-speakers or Spanish-speakers, etc.
• Protestants, Catholics, Jews, or Muslims
• Young or Old
• Pastors or Faithful
• Staff or Members

INCLUDE!

NOW, MAKE YOUR OWN LIST OF PEOPLE **YOU** WOULD RECRUIT!

YOU	TARGET	ORGANIZATION	BY WHEN	ADDRESS	TEL.	COMMENTS

c. "Door-Knocking"

TAP
TAP

THIS IS
BREAD-AND-BUTTER
RECRUITMENT!

BUT *WHAT*
SHOULD
I *SAY*?

ALWAYS USE . . .

The Magic Formula

WHO WE ARE

WHAT (THE ISSUE OR EVENT)

WHY

WE NEED **YOU**

Q & A

GET A

COMMITMENT

AFTER INTRODUCTIONS:

WHO. WE ARE . . . SPONSORED BY . . . PAST SUCCESS . . . *WE'RE GREAT!*

WHAT. THE ISSUE OR EVENT, including *WHERE* and *WHEN.*

WHY. *THE <u>ISSUE</u> IS <u>GREAT!</u>* (THINK HARD: WHY IS THIS ISSUE IMPORTANT *<u>TO THEM</u>*— NOT TO YOU?! EXPLAIN IN TERMS OF *THEIR SELF-INTEREST*.)

THINK POSITIVE!

—WE'RE GOING TO *WIN*! FUN! ADVENTURE!

WE NEED YOU!

—YOU'RE GREAT!

—WE NEED YOU *BECAUSE* . . .

(not just 'bodies' to 'cover chairs'!)

Q&A

—ANY QUESTIONS? . . . ,
PROBLEMS? SUGGESTIONS?
Listen carefully for *issues*.

—LOOK FOR:

• *TALENTS*  type?

• *CONTACTS* —"Who else can join us?"

—HAND OUT A FLIER.

GET A COMMITMENT.

—RECRUITING IS MORE THAN INVITING.

. . . SIGN 'EM UP!

Afterward . . .

1. NOTES: Write the person's name, address, phone number, talents, etc. on your list or a card. Keep a file.

2. FOLLOW UP: Stay in contact.

d. Interviews* (HOUSE VISITS)

Door-knocking is recruiting with a *brief visit*.
Interviews recruit with *longer visits*.

WHEN?

- Got *lots of time* to recruit?
- Want to make a *fresh start* in the neighborhood?
- Want to build *solid relationships* for the future?

Then use the powerful tool of INTERVIEWS!

WHY? The real purpose of an interview is to:
BUILD A RELATIONSHIP with the person.

These interviews are also great for learning what people are concerned about and to get leads on more people to contact.

BEFORE THE VISIT

1. MAKE A LIST AND A SCHEDULE.

(See pages 31–32.) Get help from a trusted neighborhood leader—say, the pastor. Find out a little about those you will visit.

- *One* or *two* persons can go on an interview.

2. PHONE AND MAKE AN APPOINTMENT.

- *INTRODUCE* YOURSELF. (Don't mention your organization or your issues!)
- Tell WHO *RECOMMENDED* YOU. "The pastor said you'd be a person who could tell me a lot about neighborhood problems." (This helps the person trust you.)
- Tell *WHY* YOU WANT TO MEET: ". . . to find out about problems in the neighborhood and how *you* feel about them." (Forget *your* issues. You want them to hear what's on *their* mind.)
- *HOW LONG?* Tell them the visit will take just a half hour—forty-five minutes at most.

---

*Ernie Cortes of I.A.F. is often credited with refining this technique.

3. HAVE A *FOLLOW-UP GOAL* FOR EACH INTERVIEW.

For example:

- A second, follow-up interview! (A great idea. Remember, you want to build a working relationship.)
- "Come to our next action/meeting."
- "Join the voter registration campaign."

Before long, **gather** those you have interviewed to share problems and plans.

DURING THE VISIT

1. "HELLO!"

BE WARM AND *FRIENDLY*. Start with what interests them:
a picture of the family, sports, the house, the parish or congregation.

2. WHY WE'RE HERE.

"We are concerned about the problems in the community.
The pastor says you can tell us a lot about what is going on."
(Forget your organization unless they ask.)

3. LISTEN . . . LISTEN . . . LISTEN . . .

They should do most of the talking.
(Nobody ever listens to them.)
Let them talk the whole time if they want.
You help by asking questions.

"What do you think about the neighborhood?
. . . about the parish? . . . about X?"
"Why are things this way?"
"What can be done about X, Y, and Z?"

Tell them you understand and sympathize.
Be on the lookout for **ISSUES**.

4. GET A FOLLOW-UP COMMITMENT.

Try to get a commitment for follow-up—
especially another interview (see above).
Use the MAGIC FORMULA now, if appropriate, ☞

| WHO |
| WHAT |
| WHY |
| YOU |
| Q&A |
| COMMIT. |

- Ask for *NAMES* of others you should visit . . .
- End with a warm *"THANKS!"*
- Leave a flier or information card.

AFTER THE VISIT

1. NOTES.

Issues, talents, friends,
commitments, follow-up.

AND

2. FOLLOW-UP.

Soon! Interviews raise high expectations.
Gather these people.

e. Speaking to a Group

We mean: addressing a church society, community group, etc.
(pulpit announcements, too, with a few changes).

BEFORE . . .   Contact the group's leader to get on the agenda of the next meeting (but not at the *end* of the meeting). Ask for enough time (5, 10, 15 minutes?).

AT THE MEETING . . .   Get to know leaders informally. When it's your turn to speak, *go to the front of the room* to where the group leader speaks. *Never* speak while seated or from an aisle.

Here's your speech. Yep, it's the MAGIC FORMULA again. Write out an outline (at least). Pages 34–35 will help.

---

1. **WHO** you and your group are . . .

2. **WHAT** the issue is . . . *WHERE & WHEN*.

3. **WHY** it's so important . . .

4. WE NEED **YOU** because . . . (give out *fliers* about now . . .)

5. **QUESTIONS & ANSWERS**

6. GET A **COMMITMENT:** sign-up sheet with name & phone number.

Be sure your presentation is clear, clean, brief, to the point.

AFTER . . .   Thank the leader(s).
Call the people who signed up and remind them to come.

38

STEP 3: PICKING AN ISSUE TO WORK ON

FOR US TO WORK ON, AN ISSUE MUST BE:

 ☐ # URGENT. That is, it must be *strongly felt* by *lots* of people. It gets people *mad.* So we can get A LOT OF PEOPLE to work on this. (If you choose an issue, you will soon have to TEST the issue in the community.)

 ☐ # WINNABLE. Do we have the necessary *strategy* and *resources*? Will this campaign exhaust people?

 ☐ # CONCRETE & SPECIFIC. This will help us to DRAMATIZE the issue. Important: An ISSUE is not a vague and general problem. It's a concrete and specific *part* of the problem. It's a handle we can grab on to. (See next page.)

 ☐ SOMETHING WHICH WILL HELP US **BUILD AN ORGANIZATION.** It will attract different groups of the neighborhood without dividing them.

... getting Concrete & Specific* ...

"Corruption!" "Drugs!" "Housing!"—serious problems but still too *vague* and *general* to work on.

Force yourselves to clarify together:

WHO IS DOING (OR NOT DOING) SOMETHING?

WHAT ARE THEY DOING (OR NOT DOING)?

TO WHOM ARE THEY DOING (OR NOT DOING) THIS? (the *victims*)

WHERE ARE THEY DOING (OR NOT DOING) IT?

FOR EXAMPLE:

WHO?: The City (County) Housing Department . . .

WHAT?: Is not providing basic services . . .

TO WHOM?: To the tenants . . .

WHERE?: Of city-owned buildings at 1197 Nelson and 3328 Third Ave.

EXERCISE: *NOW, CHOOSE YOUR OWN ISSUE, AND FILL OUT THE FOLLOWING CHART.*

WHO	WHAT	TO WHOM	WHERE

NOTE: Now ask yourselves, Is the WHO just the *cause* of the problem (say, drug dealers), or is the WHO also those (say, the police, the courts, or others) responsible to *solve* the problem? If necessary, rewrite the problem so that the WHO becomes the ones who can and should solve the problem. (That can change the WHAT completely!)

---

*Based on Harry Fagan, *Empowerment*.

Spelling Out Your Demands

YOUR ISSUE CRYSTALLIZES IN YOUR DEMANDS.

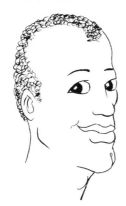

As you learn more about the issue through action and research (that's next!), spell out your demands—that is, EXACTLY WHAT YOU WANT. Your demands have to be specific, winnable and easy to understand so you can use them to recruit people to the cause.

Here are some examples of well-carved demands:

1. No more strip mining in Lincoln County! A 2% tax on all extracted minerals!

2. Two crossing guards at P.S. 41, Mon.–Fri. 8:00 to 8:30 A.M. and 2:00 to 3:00 P.M.

3. Repair all street lights in the Hunts Point neighborhood.

4. Foot patrol by police at the following three banks on the first of the month.

5. Fire the Housing Commissioner!

6. Save Engine Company 41! Fund the firehouse!

7. All political appointees off the school board!

8. _____

9. _____

As you go along, your demands may change, but they will help *focus* all your activities. . . .

STEP 4: RESEARCH THE ISSUE

Research

People + (Information) = Power

You are *detectives* and your case is a community problem.

This section has EXERCISES. Use as your case the issue you have chosen to work on—or make one up (keep it simple!):

- Suppose your landlord is not supplying heat and hot water to tenants in your building and the one next door.

- Or suppose it's a city-owned building, and the city is the culprit.

- Or suppose your community has no place where children can play safely.

There are just two things to figure out:

What **INFO** do we need?	**WHERE** can we get it?	

This is our focus. It will help to create a Group Research Plan like the one on the next page. (The above columns are the first two columns of the Plan.)

Group Research Plan

INFO	WHERE	WHO	WHEN
A. About WHAT IS HAPPENING: _____ _____ _____ _____ _____ _____ _____ _____	Interview whom? Library where? Which study?	Lydia Betsy David	March 1 March 15
B. About WHO IS RESPONSIBLE: _____ _____ _____ _____ _____ _____ _____ _____	**FIRST, LET'S FIGURE OUT WHAT WE NEED TO KNOW!**		April 1 March 1

EXERCISE A: List the *QUESTIONS* you have to ask about WHAT IS HAPPENING.

EXERCISE B: List the *QUESTIONS* you have to ask about WHO IS RESPONSIBLE.

On the next pages we deal with Column 2, "Where."

Don't forget to fill out these columns, too!

Now, *WHERE* do we get this information?

Group Research Plan

INFO	WHERE	WHO	WHEN

1. Your most important tool is—**YOUR MOUTH.**

2. SOURCES OF INFORMATION:
   Your most important sources are—
   PEOPLE WITH EXPERIENCE

SOURCES
CLOSE
TO YOU

a. **VICTIMS.**

b. **ACTIVISTS.** Find out who's already
   worked on this issue.

FARTHER
AWAY
FROM YOU
They're
important,
too.

c. **POWER.** (landlord, utility officials, police, etc.)

d. **EXPERTS.** alive: professors, etc.
   dead: books, studies.

LET'S
FILL IN
COLUMN 2

EXERCISE C: Using your list of questions from Exercise A (last page),
make a list of *WHERE* you'll go for the answers.
Visit whom? Read what?

EXERCISE D: Do the same with the *WHO* exercise (Exercise B).

(Thanks to Harry Fagan, *Empowerment,* for some good ideas on these two pages.)

Interviewing Your Sources

Before: List what you need to know.
Decide who asks what questions and who takes notes.

During: Ask before you use a tape recorder.

After: Write up a report; share it with your group.

INTERVIEWING PEOPLE IN POWER.

1. **Develop contact *inside* the organization.** Lower-level workers often want to help you.

2. **Don't be intimidated.** Be *sure* of yourself. Not nasty or arrogant—but don't beg. Be firm. Don't accept stalling and smokescreens. ("We can't give you that information." "We don't know.") Don't give up. If they continue to refuse you vital information, make *that* your group's issue: "We want that information!"

3. **The law is on your side.** Most states have a freedom of information law which protects your right to information held by state **and local** government. For example, New York State's sweeping FOI law recognizes citizens' legal right to a copy of **any document held by *any* state or local government body**—except for common-sense things like exam questions, information that could endanger someone or jeopardize a criminal investigation, and so on. Find out about FOI in your state.

HARD DATA.

Remember: You must *document your facts* if you expect to use them when *negotiating* or with the *media.*

WRITTEN INFO.

Keep an **ORGANIZED FILE** of important information about your community. Step #1, Exploring the Neighborhood, lists some, but your research will take you deeper.

Your public library and local government itself will probably provide maps and basic data about government agencies and services. Ask at the library about profiles of office-holders and directories and organizational charts of public agencies.

Learn where to go to find public records (1) of real estate ownership, taxes, and mortgages, (2) of civil and criminal court records, and (3) of incorporation records telling who owns and controls the businesses that affect your community.

STEP 5: STRATEGY—PLAN YOUR CAMPAIGN

Strategy means a **plan**—like a plan for your vacation, or to win the war or the big game. You must have a plan to win.

You want **decision-makers**, people with power, to give you something. For this you will have to focus your **POWER** (people + knowledge) to **PRESSURE** them to **NEGOTIATE** and agree to your demands. This takes several steps. These make up your **CAMPAIGN.**

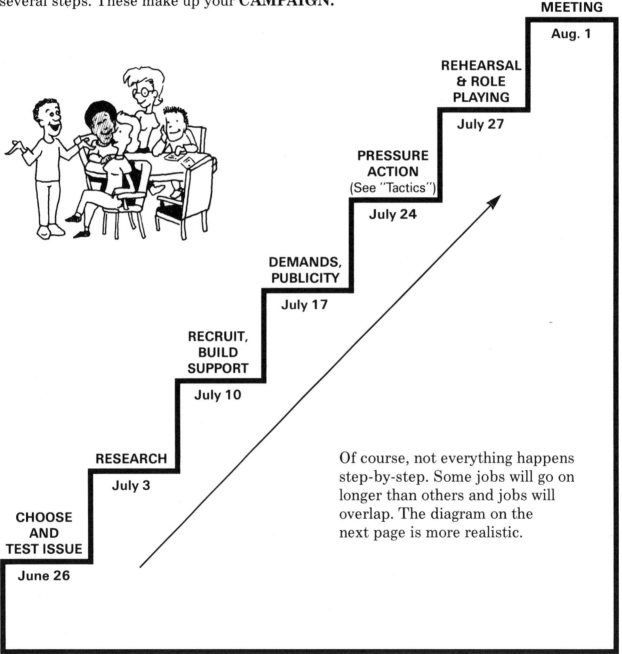

NEGOTIATION MEETING

Aug. 1

REHEARSAL & ROLE PLAYING

July 27

PRESSURE ACTION
(See "Tactics")

July 24

DEMANDS, PUBLICITY

July 17

RECRUIT, BUILD SUPPORT

July 10

RESEARCH

July 3

CHOOSE AND TEST ISSUE

June 26

Of course, not everything happens step-by-step. Some jobs will go on longer than others and jobs will overlap. The diagram on the next page is more realistic.

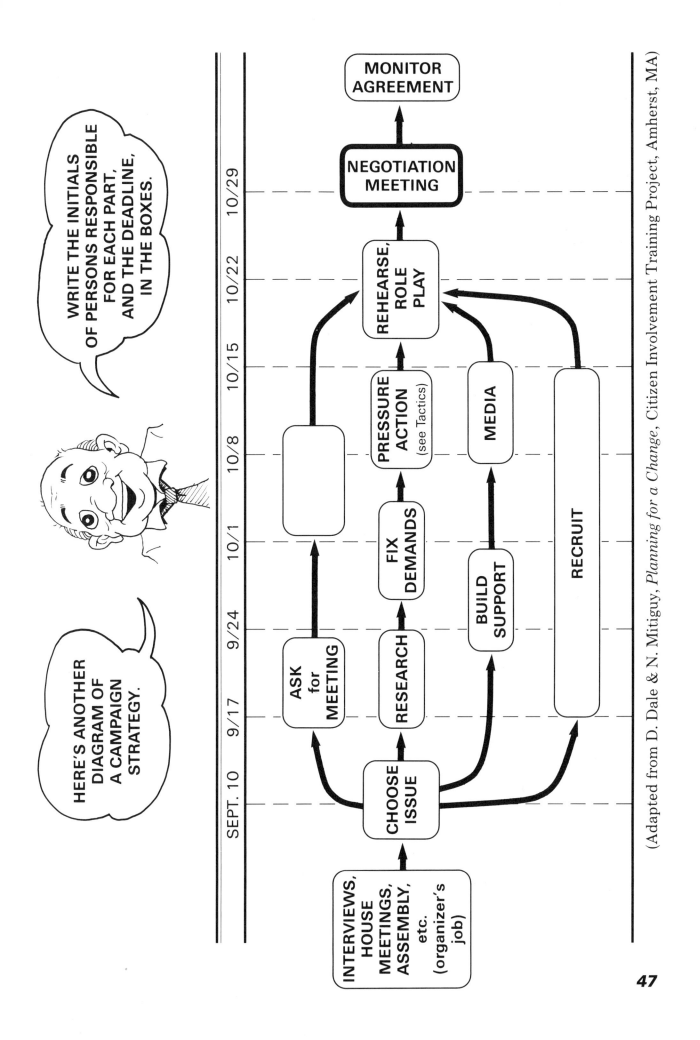

(Adapted from D. Dale & N. Mitiguy, *Planning for a Change*, Citizen Involvement Training Project, Amherst, MA)

'TARGET'-ing Decision-Makers for Negotiation

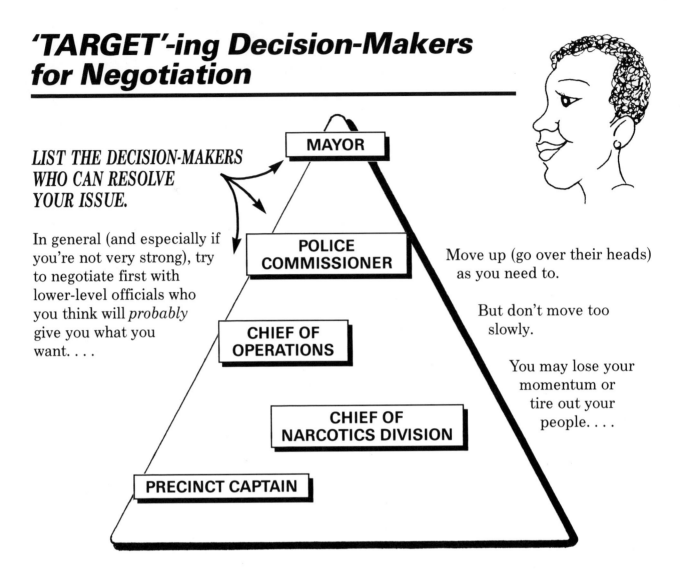

LIST THE DECISION-MAKERS WHO CAN RESOLVE YOUR ISSUE.

In general (and especially if you're not very strong), try to negotiate first with lower-level officials who you think will *probably* give you what you want. . . .

MAYOR

POLICE COMMISSIONER

CHIEF OF OPERATIONS

CHIEF OF NARCOTICS DIVISION

PRECINCT CAPTAIN

Move up (go over their heads) as you need to.

But don't move too slowly.

You may lose your momentum or tire out your people. . . .

Pressuring the Powerful

WHAT *makes this decision-maker move?*
What will make this person agree to what you want?

Power? Ambition?
Recognition? Praise?
Bad/good publicity?
Integrity? ("Decent people are suffering!")
No rent money?
Disruption of business-as-usual?
Votes?

Your answers will guide your **pressure-actions** (see "Tactics," Step 8a).

WHO *makes this decision-maker move?*
Who can influence this person?
To whom must he or she answer?

Voters?
The mayor?
Bankers, real estate people?
Church leaders?

These answers will affect how you **build support** (Step #6).

STEP 6: GETTING SUPPORT FOR YOUR CAMPAIGN

POWER = PEOPLE + KNOWLEDGE.

Now you want to enlarge the circle of people. Remember, "people" means **"constituency"** and includes **groups and organizations.** You want their backing.

SUPPORT FROM WHOM?

Make a list of those who will support the campaign, especially those who can influence decision-makers you want to meet with.

- **COMMUNITY GROUPS** (See "Exploring the Neighborhood," Step 1, above):
    - **Service Agencies**
    - **Tenant Associations**
    - **Block Clubs**
    - **Merchant Associations**
    - **PTAs**
- **COMMUNITY LEADERS**
- **POLITICIANS**
- **CHURCHES**
- **UNIVERSITIES**

Meet with **leaders** of organizations and groups—even if you don't agree with them 100% of the time. You're not marrying them, just taking them to the dance! And don't invite them; *recruit* them! (Step #2, above.)

WHAT DO WE WANT?

- **A SUPPORT LETTER**
- **ATTEND THE ACTION**
- **GET OUT THEIR TROOPS**
- **PHONE CALLS TO DECISION-MAKERS**

Note: These supporters become your **allies.** They support **your** campaign. So you still control strategy and tactics.

You could go a step further and form a **coalition** with other groups. Then it becomes the **coalition's** campaign. All groups gain power, but your group must share control with other coalition groups. Be more careful about forming coalitions than about recruiting allies. (Harry Fagan, *Empowerment,* p. 54.)

STEP 7: PUBLICITY (INCLUDING THE MEDIA)

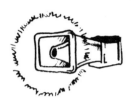

GET THE WORD OUT:

1. To get people to a public event (this page).

2. To tell the world what you're doing (next page).

1. Publicize an Upcoming Event

(GET PEOPLE TO COME TO YOUR HOUSING RALLY.)

A. **PERSONAL CONTACT** is always the single most important way to recruit.

B. **Posters** and **banners** (early—say, two weeks in advance; posters, eye-level near doors, away from other announcements),

   fliers (see below for posters and fliers),

   announcements in churches and at meetings.

C. *Using THE MEDIA*

1. Send an **announcement** to **newspapers** (c/o city desk or community calendar) ten days before you want the publicity to appear. Use the same heading (top of page) as the news release on page 53, below. Then be brief and clear: WHO (we are), WHAT, WHERE, WHEN, WHY. Graphics and color get attention. (You may also include a news release or fact sheet.) Follow up with a phone call or visit for confirmation.

2. When writing **public service announcements** for **TV or radio,** follow the above, except:

   Type your PSA triple-space in capital letters for easy reading by an announcer.

   Start with a catchy statement or question. Then: WHO, WHAT, etc. and maybe a contact PHONE NUMBER. Finally, *repeat* the WHERE and WHEN (phone number).

   Send the PSA with a brief cover letter to the Public Service Director of the station. Follow up to confirm.

2. Tell the World About Your Issue (or Event)

Publicize yesterday's great housing rally! Put pressure on city housing officials; help recruit people to the cause. The truth is the power of the poor. Some events are organized *only* to get the truth out.

A. Send the media a **notice** about ten days before the event. Crisp and clear: WHO, WHAT, WHEN, WHERE, WHY. (This will go in their file for the date of the action.) Note: A TV station wants to know if you'll have a great *picture* to film.

B. Choose **spokespersons** and prepare them to speak to reporters at the event. They should be ready to answer three questions: Who are you? Why are you here? What will you do next? (Harry Fagan). Everyone should steer spokespersons to reporters at the event.

C. Prepare a **news release** to distribute to reporters at the event (see below).

D. **Phone or visit** stations and newspapers one or two days before the event to get reporters to the action.

E. The day of the event, **phone again to confirm.**

Note 1: Compile a good **directory** (address, phone number) of all media outlets in your area. Develop *personal contacts*. Find out who are sympathetic in news organizations and get to know them. Provide background info (a press kit) on your organization. Visit.

Note 2: Get a reputation for **telling the truth.** Don't lie; don't exaggerate.

Note 3: Beware of *Friday*! Friday events are often poorly covered, and few people notice Saturday news reports. On Saturdays, though, reporters are looking around for events to cover. *Saturday* is a good day to act.

Preparing a Flier...

... Crisp and clear. The more important the information, the more it should stand out.

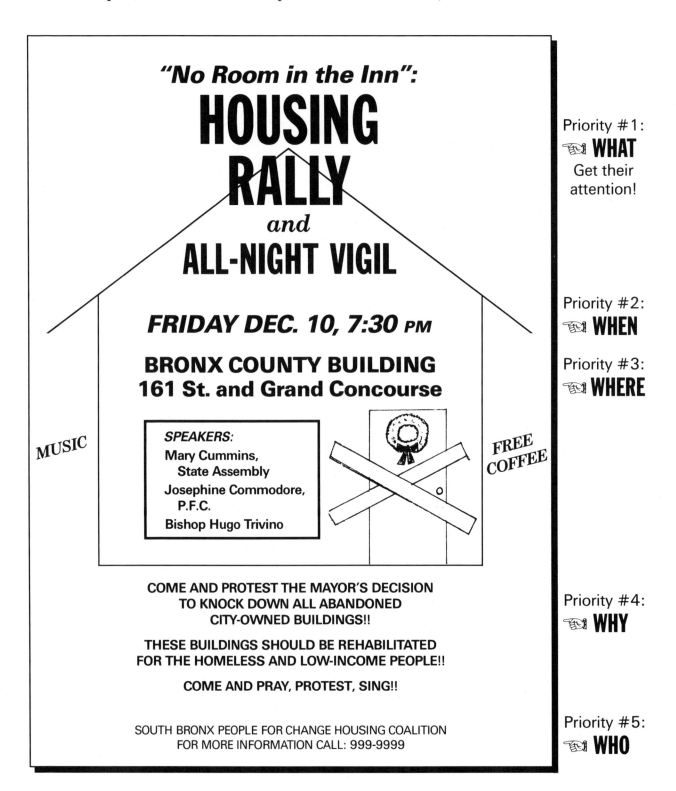

"No Room in the Inn":

HOUSING RALLY

and

ALL-NIGHT VIGIL

FRIDAY DEC. 10, 7:30 PM

BRONX COUNTY BUILDING
161 St. and Grand Concourse

MUSIC

SPEAKERS:
Mary Cummins,
   State Assembly
Josephine Commodore,
P.F.C.
Bishop Hugo Trivino

FREE COFFEE

COME AND PROTEST THE MAYOR'S DECISION
TO KNOCK DOWN ALL ABANDONED
CITY-OWNED BUILDINGS!!

THESE BUILDINGS SHOULD BE REHABILITATED
FOR THE HOMELESS AND LOW-INCOME PEOPLE!!

COME AND PRAY, PROTEST, SING!!

SOUTH BRONX PEOPLE FOR CHANGE HOUSING COALITION
FOR MORE INFORMATION CALL: 999-9999

Priority #1:
☞ **WHAT**
Get their attention!

Priority #2:
☞ **WHEN**

Priority #3:
☞ **WHERE**

Priority #4:
☞ **WHY**

Priority #5:
☞ **WHO**

Preparing a News Release . . .

HERE'S HOW . . .

1. Study the sample press release to the right. Include all the elements at the top (headline optional). Use your group's letterhead.

2. The first paragraph should briefly state all the main facts: WHO, WHAT, WHERE, WHEN, and WHY. It should be an attention-grabber like your headline. Spend a lot of time on both. If they're no good, your release winds up in the trash.

3. Go from most important to least important facts. Editors cut stories from the bottom up.

4. Simple language, short sentences, no unnecessary words.

5. Pages of a news release (PSA, etc.) end with "- MORE -". The last page ends with "- 30 -".

Note: What would interest a TV assignment editor about the event that the news release describes?

SAMPLE NEWS RELEASE

```
                              PEOPLE FOR CHANGE
[ YOUR SNAPPY LOGO HERE ]     603 Morris Ave.
                              Bronx, NY 10451

FOR IMMEDIATE RELEASE: Dec. 10, 1991
For further information call: Mary Smythe (212) 999-9999

         BRONX VIGIL PROTESTS CITY HOUSING POLICY

     Bronx, Dec. 10. -- Thursday night a coalition of 50 churches
and local organizations held an all-night vigil at Bronx County
Headquarters to protest the city's policy on low-income housing.

     In the evening chill 800 participants heard religious
leaders, state legislators, and local citizens denounce the
mayor's decision last week to demolish all vacant city-owned
buildings. "Re-habbing vacant buildings offers the best chance
for housing the homeless and for thousands of Bronx residents
living in terrible conditions," declared Angel Rodriguez,
president of South Bronx People for Change.

     The church-affiliated organization People for Change planned
last night's vigil. The group is pressuring the city to
rehabilitate 900 vacant city-owned buildings in the Bronx. The
organization demands a meeting with the mayor to discuss a four-
point proposal approved at its annual convention last May:

     (1) An immediate halt to all demolitions . . . .

Blah, blah, blah. . . .

     At last night's vigil two residents dressed up as Joseph
and Mary, recalling the Christmas story. They led prayers and
songs under a banner announcing "No Room in the Inn." About one
hundred persons continued to vigil until dawn.

                                               - 30 -
```

STEP 8:
THE ACTION

We organize a social action campaign to pressure those in power to negotiate with community people and change their policies.

"The ACTION" here refers to all those TACTICS which pressure officials and build people power.

ACTION also includes PUBLIC MEETINGS. Negotiation often takes place right there.

Finally, ACTION includes NEGOTIATION itself.

So, Step #8 has three parts:

     a. **TACTICS** (pressure-actions),

     b. **PUBLIC MEETINGS,**

     c. **NEGOTIATION.**

a. Tactics

TACTICS are all those *actions* we take to pressure decision-makers to negotiate with us and change their policies. Here are

6 KEY PRINCIPLES:

1. RESPECT THE **DIGNITY** OF **ALL PERSONS** AND THE PRINCIPLES OF **NON-VIOLENCE**.

2. EXPOSE THE **TRUTH** (your most powerful weapon) ABOUT:
   a. WHAT THE PEOPLE ARE **SUFFERING,**
   b. THE **GOODNESS** OF THE PEOPLE,
   c. THE **IRRESPONSIBILITY** OF THEIR ADVERSARY.

3. STAY **INSIDE** THE **EXPERIENCE** OF THE **PEOPLE**.
(Sing, pray, work together, have a good time!)

GO **OUTSIDE** THE **EXPERIENCE** OF THE **ADVERSARY**.
Equalize the power situation.
Throw them off balance.
(Arrive in large numbers.
Interrupt business-as-usual.)

4. DRAMA! FUN! HUMOR!

HOUSING!

5. ESCALATE: From simple, easy tactics to riskier, more difficult tactics.

6. PREPARE AHEAD: Know what to do if "X" happens—or "Y" or "Z".
You can't prepare for everything.
Anticipate obvious problems.

TACTICS: IDEAS FOR ACTION

When you are tempted to mourn, "There's nothing we can do," recharge the batteries of your imagination. This list can help: 69 different kinds of non-violent action that have been put into practice at one time or other.*

PROTEST AND PERSUADE

PROPAGANDA AND PUBLICITY; STATEMENTS
1. Publish, circulate a written statement
2. Petitions. (You can present them dramatically.)
3. Letters to the editor
4. Press conference
5. Leaflets
6. Banners and posters
7. Public service announcements, etc. (radio, TV)

PRESSURE INDIVIDUALS AND INSTITUTIONS
8. Telephone campaign
9. Letter (postcard) campaign
10. "Fraternizing"—invite an official to lunch, to a neighborhood celebration, etc. ("humanize" yourselves in his or her eyes)
11. Lobbying
12. Visit official's office, with or without an appointment
13. Visit official's house (or club or church); picket, leaflet
14. Picketing
15. Invite a decision-maker on a neighborhood tour to see the problems.
16. Sue (in court; for example, take the landlord to court). Beware! Keep pressure on *outside* court.
17. Pressure a secondary target (i.e. someone who can in turn pressure the primary target, especially his/her boss!)

SYMBOLIC ACTIONS; DRAMA
18. Processions and marches
19. Vigils and religious services (use candles, lights, etc.)
20. Songs (comical, religious, etc.)
21. Caricatures and symbols (dummies and effigies)
22. Painting a wall, building, etc.
23. Symbolic clothing; disguises
24. Skits; street theater
25. Mock awards ("Year's Worst Public Servant")
26. Mock elections
27. Mock trial
28. Symbolic sounds (car horn, bang pots, bells, etc.)

---

*Compiled with much help from Gene Sharp, *The Politics of Nonviolent Action. Part Three: The Dynamics of Nonviolent Action* (Boston, 1973).

29. New names for streets, plazas, etc. (with signs)
30. Symbolic reclamations: plant crops or tree on land; put up a fence; sign a "lease," etc.
31. Declaration of independence: the Democratic Republic of the South Bronx, etc.
32. Symbolic (or real) funeral for victims
33. Homage at burial places
34. Destruction of *your own* property
35. Group fasting; hunger strike

PUBLIC ASSEMBLIES
36. Assemblies of protest or support
37. Teach-in
38. Public meeting (or meetings of a smaller delegation) to hold public officials or candidates accountable.

WITHDRAWAL AND RENUNCIATION
39. Walk-outs
40. Silence (after a speech)
41. Turning one's back (on a speaker)

VOTING
42. Registering voters
43. Educating voters
44. Mobilizing voters on election day

NON-COOPERATION

45. Renouncing honors
46. Rent strike
47. Boycott of public services (like the subway, buses)
48. Boycott of public agencies—even refusing benefits (e.g. welfare)
49. Refuse to help public officials (e.g. police, etc.)
50. Boycott a school
51. Boycott elections (e.g. of the tenant association)
52. Boycott private businesses (such as a supermarket chain)
53. Buy only in locally owned stores
54. Boycott a bank (withdraw all money)
55. Refusal of an assembled group to disperse when told to
56. Civil disobedience (openly and without violence) of an unjust law; seeking to be imprisoned
57. Persuading lower officials not to carry out orders but to support the public

DIRECT INTERVENTION

58. Talk (a lot) in a public meeting or hearing
59. Sit in. Take seats, especially in a small place. Timing: Christmas shopping; just before elections
60. Pray-in

61. Mill-in. People enter and leave and mill about. Timing!
62. Blocking (physically but passively) an entrance
63. Blocking traffic the same way
64. Blocking an unjust action (demolition, eviction, etc.)
65. Overloading systems. Examples:
    100 people ask medical help in the emergency room or clinic.
    100 people buy one item and stand in the supermarket checkout line.
    100 people ask change of $1.00 in the bank.
    100 people pay Con Edison with pennies.
    Telephone and letter (postcard) campaigns. Etc.
66. Land seizure
67. Squatting (taking over a building)
68. Reverse strike: to shame and pressure officials, the public does the work which the government should do but doesn't
69. Create alternative institutions: school, fire department, etc. (Careful!: This is done as a *tactic*, not a solution.)

b. Public Meetings

We will assume the public meeting *includes negotiation* with decision-makers. Make adjustments to plan for a different kind of public meeting.

I. BEFORE THE MEETING.*

The "Before" is more important than the "During," and RECRUITMENT is more important than anything else.

A. WEEK #1, MEETING #1.

1. *Decide on decision-makers* (officials) you want to negotiate with.

   Spell out the people's *proposals/demands.* (Simple.)

   Prepare next step and fallback: "What will we do after the meeting?" "What if officials refuse to come or don't show?"

2. *How many people do you want*?

3. Get a *meeting hall.* Not too big. You want it to look packed!

4. *Send invitation* to officials. Specify your proposals/demands in a *general* way. Don't make it an ambush, a total surprise; but don't give it all away either!

"To begin with, I would like to express my sincere thanks and deep appreciation for the opportunity to meet with you. While there are still profound differences between us, I think the very fact of my presence here today is a major breakthrough."

---

*The "Before" generally follows a plan developed by Ellen Ziff.

B. WEEK #2, MEETING #2.

1. Follow-up invitation to officials.

2. Discussion of agenda and format (set time limit for meeting).

   AGENDA
   - Prayer
   - Introductory statement
   - Testimony by victims
   - Negotiation of demands by negotiation team and/or questions from the floor.
   - Open time
   - Summary and call to action

3. *Recruitment* (the most important task of all!)
   - *Personal Contacts.* Also, pulpit announcements and church bulletins, posters, fliers, phone calls, public service announcements, etc. (see pages 51–53).
   - Involve as many people as possible.
   - Have each group or individual agree to recruit "X" number of people.

C. WEEK #3, NO MEETING! Do what you just planned!

D. WEEK #4, MEETING #3.

Reward those who worked in last three weeks with top jobs at the public meeting.

1. Review agenda

2. Assign leadership roles:
   - chairperson
   - negotiators, including chief negotiator
   - testimony-givers (victims)
   - attendance-takers
   - sergeant-at-arms
   - floor team
   - ushers
   - music leaders
   - pray-ers
   - spokespersons to media

3. Discussion of speeches/statements

4. Discussion of *handouts* and press packets: the issue, the official/s, etc.

5. Review recruitment assignments

6. Meeting planning assignments
   - set-up
   - keys
   - lights
   - sound
   - blackboards
   - visual aids

7. Press release, ten days in advance

E. WEEK #5, MEETING #4.

1. Role play.

2. Final review of recruitment.

3. Press calls (and press visits).

4. Mail agenda to official/s.

5. Confirm attendance of official/s one or two days before.

II. DURING THE MEETING.

A. *PREPARE THE CROWD.* Have the public show up a half hour before the officials. Sing; explain the agenda; introduce the "people's negotiating team" (get everybody's support for them); explain the issues briefly, clearly; encourage participation.

B. Have a *"FLOOR TEAM"* encouraging participation during the meeting.

C. *CONTROL THE AGENDA* and the microphone. Be fair to all, including the opposition.

D. *NEGOTIATE* well! (See below.) If helpful, turn to the public and ask their opinion of the officials' response(s) and of any compromises offered. Beware of the officials trying to split the public from leadership and negotiators!

E. *SUMMARIZE* all agreements at the end and make clear provision for follow-up.

III. AFTER THE MEETING.

A. Evaluate.

B. Send a letter to officials confirming agreements.

C. Monitor agreements and plan followup (See I, above.)

D. If appropriate, celebrate!

c. Negotiation

EVERYTHING IN THE CAMPAIGN SO FAR PREPARES FOR THIS. IT'S YOUR MOST IMPORTANT MEETING. **PREPARE WELL!!**

BEFORE . . .

1. *ROLE PLAY beforehand.*
   Anticipate the other side's response to your demands.

WHERE? . . .

2. *MEET ON YOUR TURF.* Your neighborhood. Your agenda (they can help plan it). Have as many of your people there as possible. You control the microphones.

WITH WHOM? . . .

3. *Only negotiate with DECISION-MAKERS.*
   Confirm their attendance a day or two before. Know about them—who their *boss* is, how they deal with groups like yours.

WHAT? . . .

4. *PRESENTING DEMANDS.*

   a. Present *simple* and *specific* demands: dates, times, places.

   b. Negotiate *one* demand at a time.

   c. Frame demands in a *YES or NO* way.

   d. *Prioritize* your demands. Which can you give up? Which not?

   e. Assign a *chief negotiator* and supporters for each demand.

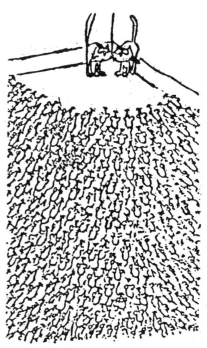

"Well, don't just stand there— negotiate!"

5. *NEGOTIATING.*
(Remember: You want a COMMITMENT on each demand.)

a. *Personalize* the issue:
   It's not "the system."
   Here are the *victims.*
   You have to change this.

b. Start with what you know
   best: *your experience.*
   Stay close to your turf.
   Victims' testimony.
   Dramatize.

c. Back it up with *facts and figures.*
   But don't get lost on their turf.
   Use visual aids.

d. Start with the *justice* of your cause
   (Martin Luther King): "It's not right!"
   The truth is your best weapon (Gandhi).

e. Back this up with your *power.*
   Remind them of your *victories, supporters.*
   "Everybody's upset about this!"

f. Think like your opponent.

g. Have *fallback* positions prepared.

h. Stay *united.* No disagreements.

i. *Caucus* (in private) when necessary.
   Expect surprises (you want two crossing guards;
   they offer one). If your people are outside, caucus with them.
   Clear all agreements first with your people.

PROBLEM (Demand)	YES	BY WHEN	NO

FOR WHAT? . . . *6. COMMITMENTS.*

> a. Your goal is always to get a
>   *COMMITMENT* on each demand.

b. Set *deadlines* for each commitment.

c. Get it in *writing* whenever possible:
   A *contract.* A joint press release.
   At least a letter of confirmation.

d. Work out a way to *monitor* the commitments:
   follow-up meetings, tours, etc.
   (This means each commitment has
   to be clear and measurable.)

e. After getting all your Yes and No answers,
   go back and work on those No's again.

f. At the end of the meeting, *review* exactly
   what has been agreed to.

LATER . . . *7. FOLLOWUP.*

a. *Publicize* the agreement.

b. *Celebrate* the victory!!

c. *Monitor the agreement!*

STEP 9: EVALUATION

Action is the real teacher. But it only teaches if we reflect on it. Evaluation is a constant process. Evaluate everything you do: recruitment, research, letter-writing campaigns, fundraising—*everything.* Sometimes evaluations are brief and informal. After important efforts, they should be extended and well-organized. Involve as many participants as you reasonably can.

We have found this simple format the most useful: First, What went **right**? List these on the left. Second, What went **Wrong**?—or, How can we **improve** this for the next time? List these on the right. Social action is hard work and important work. So it is just as important to celebrate our strengths as it is to face up squarely, and with a sense of humor, to our weaknesses.

Cover your whole plan. Stay as concrete and specific as possible. Not: "There was a good turnout," but: "We met our goal of 250 participants." Not: "Our research wasn't good enough," but: "We should have known that the uniformed police and the narcotics police are completely separate divisions."

Some touchy questions ("What happened to the rest of the money?" "Didn't Jack dominate everything?") might better be handled in a smaller, or private session. But face them!

Ask, finally: "Are we stronger? More respected? More skilled? . . . Was it worth all the effort?"

STEP 10: MONITOR THE AGREEMENT

The battle is not over when you negotiate an agreement with decision-makers. Many victories have been lost because officials made a commitment when the spotlight was on them but failed to deliver what they promised—and community people were not prepared to make them deliver. So when you negotiate a commitment, agree on the spot to a follow-up schedule (specific dates and places) to monitor delivery on the promise. Publicize the commitment. Be ready to publicize failures to deliver. Prepare to take action if decision-makers retreat on their commitment.

STEP 11: CELEBRATE!

Social action **is** hard work. But few things can destroy it faster than making it **all** business and hard work. Care for each other. Waste time together. Get to be friends. Laugh a lot, even at mistakes. Above all, **celebrate victories**—even little ones. It's amazing how people can forget, and even deny, what they have won! Celebrating keeps the victory fresh in our minds so it can carry us along when the going gets tough.